THE WHISPERING ROOM
HAUNTED POEMS

Chosen by
GILLIAN CLARKE

Illustrated by
JUSTIN TODD

Kingfisher

For Ian and Deirdre
J.T.

For Cai, Coyan, Llaima-Mali, little Cai, Ifan, and Jake
G.C.

KINGFISHER
An imprint of Larousse plc
Elsley House, 24-30 Great Titchfield Street
London W1P 7AD

First published by Kingfisher 1996
2 4 6 8 10 9 7 5 3 1

See page 72 for Acknowledgements

A CIP catalogue record for this book
is available from the British Library

ISBN 1 85697 363 8

Designed by Chris Fraser
Edited by Suzanne Carnell

Printed in Singapore

INTRODUCTION

*W*ords can make your skin prickle, words like "wraith", "phantom", "drear", "who-vering", "triptrap", "louring" and "shallop". Some words are put together in a way that makes you shiver, like "sulphurous, sunless and sinister place", "your stare goes dry", or "full fathom five".

As a child I loved to keep myself awake at night by thinking "forever and ever and ever and ever and . . .", or telling myself ghost stories, or reading mysterious poems. Scaring myself on purpose made me feel alive, like being on the most terrifying ride at the fair. While you're riding high, you scream and wish it would stop, but afterwards you remember it as the best thing you have ever felt, the stars coming close, then the ground swooping up to meet you.

A really good poem, especially a haunted poem, can make you dizzy like that, scared for a minute, then on safe ground again, remembering being up there, scared, among the stars. It's over, but you can read it again and again, and get a little frightened every time.

Poems and houses can be haunted, but so can wrecked cars, empty schools, sunken ships, clothes dancing in the wind, the waves, the woods and the weather. Haunting is all about imagination, and the best imaginers are poets and children.

GILLIAN CLARKE

WATER SPRITE

You just have to
 start blowing bubbles underwater from the crack of
  dawn,
 stir up ripples all the morning,
 at noontime run the water off your coat-tails on the
  strips between the fields,
  all afternoon tread the mud in wavy ridges,
  at dusk start croaking at the moon, —

 no one has the time today
 just to sit and do a little haunting.

MIROSLAV HOLUB

WHO?

Who is that child I see wandering, wandering
Down by the side of the quivering stream?
Why does he seem not to hear, though I call to him?
Where does he come from, and what is his name?

Why do I see him at sunrise and sunset
Taking, in old-fashioned clothes, the same track?
Why, when he walks, does he cast not a shadow
Though the sun rises and falls at his back?

Why does the dust lie so thick on the hedgerow
By the great field where a horse pulls the plough?
Why do I see only meadows, where houses
Stand in a line by the riverside now?

Why does he move like a wraith by the water,
Soft as the thistledown on the breeze blown?
When I draw near him so that I may hear him,
Why does he say that his name is my own?

CHARLES CAUSLEY

DIPPING GAME

Hinx, minx, the old witch winks,
The fat begins to fry.
No one at home but Jumping Joan,
Father, Mother and I.

Stick, stock, stone dead,
Blind men can't see.
Every knave will have a slave.
Is it you or me?

ANON

There was an old woman who lived in a wood,
and an owl at the door as sentinel stood.
Whenever the old woman wanted to wander
she rode through the air on a very fine gander.

There was an old woman who lived in an oak,
and when she went out she wore a black cloak.
Whenever she fancied she took to the sky,
riding a broomstick way up high.

There was an old woman lived under the hill,
and if she's not gone, she lives there still.

ANON

THE SPELLER'S BAG

Here a bone.
Here a stone.
In my bag
I keep them all.

A stone brought me
by the sea.
A bone taken from where
I'll never tell thee.

A bone, a stone,
a feather, a shell,
all in my bag
to cast a spell.

A shell that taught
the wind to howl.
A feather stolen
from the back of an owl.

Then again it might be
from a raven's neck.
I'll never tell thee.

Look inside all who dare.

Inside my bag
you'll find your fear.

JOHN AGARD

THE WOMAN OF WATER

There once was a woman of water
Refused a Wizard her hand.
So he took the tears of a statue
And the weight from a grain of sand
And he squeezed the sap from a comet
And the height from a cypress tree
And he drained the dark from midnight
And he charmed the brains from a bee
And he soured the mixture with thunder
And stirred it with ice from hell
And the woman of water drank it down
And she changed into a well.

There once was a woman of water
Who was changed into a well
And the well smiled up at the Wizard
And down down down that old Wizard fell . . .

ADRIAN MITCHELL

THE MAN IN THE WILDERNESS

The man in the wilderness said to me,
How many strawberries grow in the sea?
I answered him, as I thought good,
As many as herrings grow in the wood.

The man in the wilderness said to me,
How many stars in the sky? said he.
I stare at the moon till it makes me shiver
And wonder and wonder, who made Forever?

The man in the wilderness said to me,
Who's that breathing in the sycamore tree?
Who goes by on a silver hoof,
Rattling windows, tapping the roof?

When you're lying in bed at night,
What's that thing like slithery light
That slides through the curtains and down the wall,
Under the door and into the hall,

Like a flat star falling out of the sky,
Whenever a car goes driving by?
What's that ticking in the central heating?
Whose heart is that so loudly beating?

The man in the wilderness said to me,
How many buckets would empty the sea?
Who-who's that crying in the cold night air?
Who-who? Who-who? Who-who goes there?

How many strawberries? How many stars?
Herrings, owl-cries, passing cars?
How many galaxies more, or less?
Oh, go away, man in the wilderness!

GILLIAN CLARKE

THE BOGEYMAN

In the desolate depths of a perilous place
the bogeyman lurks, with a snarl on his face.
Never dare, never dare to approach his dark lair
for he's waiting . . . just waiting . . . to get you.

He skulks in the shadows, relentless and wild
in his search for a tender, delectable child.
With his steely sharp claws and his slavering jaws
oh he's waiting . . . just waiting . . . to get you.

Many have entered his dreary domain
but not even one has been heard from again.
They no doubt made a feast for the butchering beast
and he's waiting . . . just waiting . . . to get you.

In that sulphurous, sunless and sinister place
he'll crumple your bones in his bogey embrace.
Never never go near if you hold your life dear,
for oh! . . . what he'll do . . . when he gets you!

JACK PRELUTSKY

THE GHOST OF CAUPOLICÁN

Who is this,
like the tiger,
riding the wind
with his phantom-like body?
When the oaks see him,
when the people see him,
they speak with hushed voices,
saying one to another:
"Lo, brother, there is
the ghost of Caupolicán."

ARAUCANIAN INDIAN
SONG

THEME IN YELLOW

I spot the hills
With yellow balls in autumn.
I light the prairie cornfields
Orange and tawny gold clusters
And I am called pumpkins.
On the last of October
When dusk is fallen
Children join hands
And circle round me
Singing ghost songs
And love to the harvest moon:
I am a jack-o'-lantern
With terrible teeth
And the children know
I am fooling.

CARL SANDBURG

FULL MOON

Full moon is the nicest time
For telling 'Nancy story
Except the ones 'bout snake and ghost
Because they are so scary

Hide and seek is nice then too
Because it's light as day
And mamas don't say it's too late
If you go out to play

ODETTE THOMAS

ANANCY

Anancy is a spider;
Anancy is a man;
Anancy's West Indian
And West African.

Sometimes, he wears a waistcoat;
Sometimes, he carries a cane;
Sometimes, he sports a top-hat;
Sometimes, he's just a plain
Ordinary, black, hairy spider.

Anancy is vastly cunning,
Tremendously greedy,
Excessively charming,
Hopelessly dishonest,
Warmly loving,
Firmly confident,
Fiercely wild,
A fabulous character,
Completely out of our mind
And out of his, too.

Anancy is a master planner,
A great user
Of other people's plans;
He pockets everybody's food,
Shelter, land, money, and more;
He achieves mountains of things,
Like stolen flour dumplings;
He deceives millions of people,
Even the man in the moon;
And he solves all the mysteries
On earth, in air, under sea.

And always,
Anancy changes
From a spider into a man
And from a man into a spider
And back again
At the drop of a sleepy eyelid.

ANDREW SALKEY

NIGHT

There's a dark, dark wood
inside my head
where the night owl cries;
where clambering roots
catch at my feet
where fox and bat
and badger meet
and night has eyes.

There's a dark, dark wood
inside my head
of oak and ash and pine;
where the clammy grasp
of a beaded web
can raise the hairs
on a wanderer's head
as he stares alone
from his mossy bed
and feels
the chill of his spine.

There's a dark, dark wood
inside my head
where the spider weaves;
where the rook rests
and the pale owl nests,
where moonlit bracken
spikes the air
and the moss is covered,
layer upon layer,
by a thousand fallen leaves.

JUDITH NICHOLLS

FAIRY STORY

I went into the wood one day
And there I walked and lost my way

When it was so dark I could not see
A little creature came to me

He said if I would sing a song
The time would not be very long

But first I must let him hold my hand tight
Or else the wood would give me a fright

I sang a song, he let me go
But now I am home again there is nobody I know.

STEVIE SMITH

VOICES

I heard those voices today again:
Voices of women and children, down in that hollow
Of blazing light into which swoops the tree-darkened lane
Before it mounts up into the shadow again.

I turned the bend – just as always before
There was no one at all down there in the sunlit hollow;
Only ferns in the wall, foxgloves by the hanging door
Of that blind old desolate cottage. And just as before

I noticed the leaping glitter of light
Where the stream runs under the lane; in that mine-dark archway
– Water and stones unseen as though in the gloom of night –
Like glittering fish slithers and leaps the light.

I waited long at the bend of the lane,
But heard only the murmuring water under the archway.
Yet I tell you, I've been to that place again and again,

And always, in summer weather, those voices are plain,
Down near that broken house, just where the tree-darkened lane
Swoops into the hollow of light before mounting to shadow again.

FRANCES BELLERBY

ALONE IN THE DARK

She has taken out the candle,
She has left me in the dark;
From the window not a glimmer,
From the fireplace not a spark.

I am frightened as I'm lying
All alone here in my bed,
And I've wrapped the clothes as closely
As I can around my head.

But what is it makes me tremble?
And why should I fear the gloom?
I am certain there is nothing
In the corners of the room.

ANON

THE OTHER LIFE

The teddy bear is six foot tall,
it scrapes its head on the ceiling.
At night it unzippers its furry skin,
steps out bare as a sheared sheep,
to move with night echoes,
slow shadows, a cold silentness.

One night out walking
he met fire who scorched his
    amber fur,
fed on his soft stuffing,
left a husk of debris,
soot on his footprints.

SUE MOULES

THERE WAS A LADY

There was a lady all skin and bone,
The skinniest lady ever known.
It happened on a certain day
The lady went to church to pray.

When she came to the church stile
She rested for a little while.
When she came to the churchyard,
There the ringing bells she heard.

When she came to the church door,
She stopped to rest a little more.
When at last she went inside,
The parson preached on sin and pride.

She looked up, and she looked down
And saw a skeleton on the ground.
In the bony skull, on its bony chin
The worms crawled out, the worms crawled in.

Then she to the parson said,
Will I be a skeleton when I'm dead?
Oh, yes, oh, yes, the parson said,
You'll be like that when you are dead.

ANON

O o - o o - A H - A H !

A woman in a churchyard sat,
Oo-oo-ah-ah!
Very short and very fat,
Oo-oo-ah-ah!
She saw three corpses carried in,
Oo-oo-ah-ah!
Very tall and very thin,
Oo-oo-ah-ah!

ANON

A SWEEP OF GHOSTS

In the graveyard at night
when the full moon's bright,
you may see something scary moo-vering.
Don't scream or yell,
or clang the church bell
because it's only the ghosties whoo-vering!

JOHN RICE

There is the story of a deserted island
where five men walked down to the bay.

The story of this island is
that three men would two men slay.

Three men dug two graves in the sand,
three men stood on the sea wet rock,
three shadows moved away.

There is the story of a deserted island
where three men walked down to the bay.

The story of this island is
that two men would one man slay.

Two men dug one grave in the sand,
two men stood on the sea wet rock,
two shadows moved away.

There is the story of a deserted island
where two men walked down to the bay.

The story of this island is
that one man would one man slay.

One man dug one grave in the sand,
one man stood on the sea wet rock,
one shadow moved away.

There is the story of a deserted island
where four ghosts walked down to the bay.

The story of this island is
that four ghosts would one man slay.

Four ghosts dug one grave in the sand,
four ghosts stood on the sea wet rock;
five ghosts moved away.

DANNIE ABSE

27

THE TITANIC

Under the ocean, where water falls
over the decks and tilted walls
where the sea comes knocking at the great ship's door,
the band still plays
to the drum of the waves,
to the drum of the waves.

Down in the indigo depths of the sea
the white shark waltzes gracefully
down the water-stairway, across the ballroom floor
where the cold shoals flow,
and ghost dancers go,
ghost dancers go.

Their dresses are frayed, their shoes are lost,
their jewels and beads and bones are tossed
into the sand, all turned to stone,
as they sing in the sea
eternally,
eternally.

Currents comb their long loose hair,
dancers sway forever where
the bright fish nibble their glittering bones,
till they fall asleep
in the shivering deep,
in the shivering deep.

GILLIAN CLARKE

SONG OF THE FISHING GHOSTS

Night is the time when phantoms play,
  Flows the river,
  Phantoms white
  Phantoms black
Fish in the dark salt water bay.

Skulls are nets for phantom fishers,
  Flows the river,
Phantoms red on a phantom river
  Dark flows the river.

Black phantom splashes
  Flows the river
White phantom splashes
  Flows the river.

Night is the time when phantoms play,
  Heads are nets
  For phantom fishers
There on the dark salt water bay.

  Phantoms black
  Phantoms red
  Phantoms white
  For nets their heads
And the dark, dark, dark river flows.

EFUA SUTHERLAND

MAMA-WATA

Down by the seaside
when the moon is in bloom
sits Mama-Wata
gazing up at the moon

She sits as she combs
her hair like a loom
she sits as she croons
a sweet kind of tune

But don't go near Mama-Wata
when the moon is in bloom
for sure she will take you
down to your doom.

GRACE NICHOLS

SEA MONSTER

Calm, empty sea
So soothes your eye
"Such peace!" you sigh –

Suddenly ME!

So huge, so near,
So really here,
Your stare goes dry
To see me come

So like a swan,
So slow, so high
You cannot cry

Already gone
Completely numb.

TED HUGHES

ARIEL'S SONG

Full fathom five thy father lies;
    Of his bones are coral made;
Those are pearls that were his eyes:
    Nothing of him that doth fade,
But doth suffer a sea-change
Into something rich and strange:
Sea-nymphs hourly ring his knell.
    Ding-dong!
Hark! now I hear them,
    Ding-dong, bell!

WILLIAM SHAKESPEARE

from *THE SEA*

The sea is a hungry dog,
Giant and grey.
He rolls on the beach all day.
With his clashing teeth and shaggy jaws
Hour upon hour he gnaws
The rumbling, tumbling stones,
And "Bones, bones, bones, bones!"
The giant sea-dog moans,
Licking his greasy paws.

JAMES REEVES

THE BONES OF THE VASA

I saw the bones of the *Vasa* knit in the moonlight
I heard her hull creak as the salt sea slapped it
I smelled her tar and her freshly-planed pine,

there were rye loaves slung up on poles for drying
there were herrings in barrels and brandy-wine
and every plank in her body was singing,

off-duty sailors were throwing the dice
while the royal flag cracked at the mast
and the wind grew strong and the clouds flew past

Oh the *Vasa* never set sail down the salt sea's stream
down the salt stream for a second time
while the midsummer islands waited like secrets,

the King's *Vasa* flew down like a swan
parting the waves and the sea's furrow
parting that long road where the drowned roll
and the tide rules the kingdom of no one.

HELEN DUNMORE

(The *Vasa* *was a royal Swedish ship of the sixteenth century.*
She sank on her maiden voyage.)

THE VISITOR

A crumbling churchyard, the sea and the moon;
The waves had gouged out grave and bone;
A man was walking, late and alone . . .

He saw a skeleton on the ground;
A ring on a bony hand he found.

He ran home to his wife and gave her the ring.
"Oh, where did you get it?" He said not a thing.

"It's the loveliest ring in the world," she said,
As it glowed on her finger. They skipped off to bed.

At midnight they woke. In the dark outside,
"Give me my ring!" a chill voice cried.

"What was that, William? What did it say?"
"Don't worry, my dear. It'll soon go away."

"I'm coming!" A skeleton opened the door.
"Give me my ring!" It was crossing the floor.

"What was that, William? What did it say?"
"Don't worry, my dear. It'll soon go away."

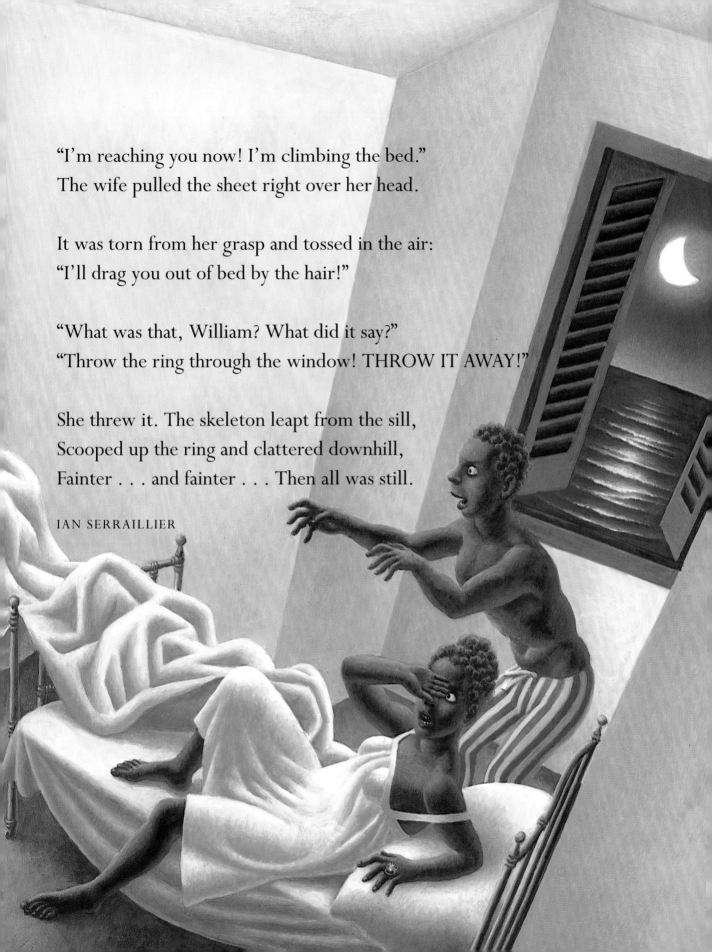

"I'm reaching you now! I'm climbing the bed."
The wife pulled the sheet right over her head.

It was torn from her grasp and tossed in the air:
"I'll drag you out of bed by the hair!"

"What was that, William? What did it say?"
"Throw the ring through the window! THROW IT AWAY!"

She threw it. The skeleton leapt from the sill,
Scooped up the ring and clattered downhill,
Fainter . . . and fainter . . . Then all was still.

IAN SERRAILLIER

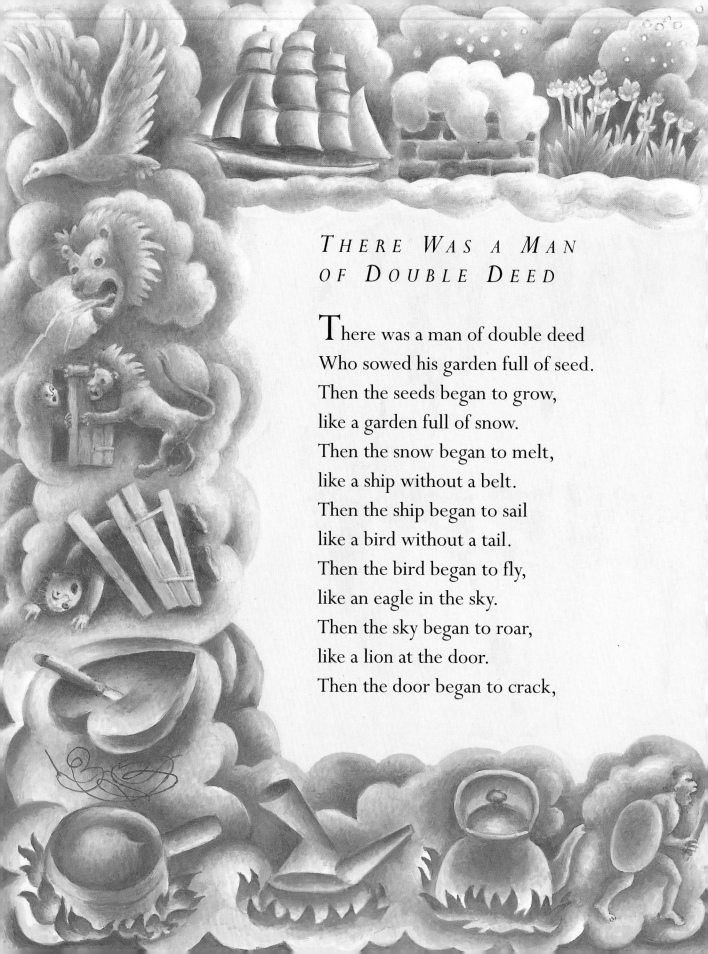

THERE WAS A MAN OF DOUBLE DEED

There was a man of double deed
Who sowed his garden full of seed.
Then the seeds began to grow,
like a garden full of snow.
Then the snow began to melt,
like a ship without a belt.
Then the ship began to sail
like a bird without a tail.
Then the bird began to fly,
like an eagle in the sky.
Then the sky began to roar,
like a lion at the door.
Then the door began to crack,

like a stick across my back.
Then my back began to smart,
like a penknife in my heart.
Then my heart began to bleed,
like a needle full of thread.
Then the thread began to rot,
like a turnip in the pot.
Then the pot began to boil,
like a bottle full of oil.
Then the oil began to settle,
like the water in the kettle.
When the kettle boils no more,
Out goes the man to fight a war.

ANON

THE OLD CLOCK HOUSE

The old house remembers,
Its master, its master.
The one that made clocks,
Old clocks of those days.
But one day, one dark day,
The old Master died.
So the old house and
The clock on the front
Trembled and cried,
They cried for their Master,
    the master.
They whispered,
Yes, whispered, saying:
Hope someone comes
To sing away sorrow.
For more than two years
The clock house fell silent
Then a lady I know came
To live in that house,
The glad house, and she
Came to sing away sorrow . . .
Forever . . .

MARTA JADWIGA CIECHANOWICZ
(Aged 9)

GREEN CANDLES

"There's someone at the door," said gold candlestick;
"Let her in, let her in quick!"
"There is a small hand groping at the handle:
Why don't you turn it?" asked green candle.

"Don't go, don't go," said the Heppelwhite chair,
"lest you find a strange lady there."
"Yes, stay where you are," whispered the white wall:
"there is nobody there at all."

"I know her little foot," grey carpet said:
"Who but I should know her light tread?"
"She shall come in," answered the open door,
"and not," said the room, "go out any more."

HUMBERT WOLFE

QUIETER THAN SNOW

I went to school a day too soon
And couldn't understand
Why silence hung in the yard like sheets
Nothing to flap or spin, no creaks
Or shocks of voices, only air.

And the carpark empty of teachers' cars
Only the first September leaves
Dropping like paper. No racks of bikes
No kicking legs, no fights,
No voices, laughter, anything.

Yet the door was open. My feet
Sucked down the corridor. My reflection
Walked with me past the hall.
My classroom smelt of nothing. And the silence
Rolled like thunder in my ears.

At every desk a still child stared at me
Teachers walked through walls and back again
Cupboard doors swung open, and out crept
More silent children, and still more.

They tiptoed round me
Touched me with ice-cold hands
And opened up their mouths with laughter
That was

Quieter than snow.

BERLIE DOHERTY

CAT LANE

Fog lives here. It slinks against walls,
lithe, muscled, never heard.
A drainpipe ticks in the yard,
each drop wobbling as it falls.

No one in the dark nights of November
comes down here to the overflowing bins.
Wet posters peel softly from palings;
even the rain has claws.

Slot between houses, dark, star-hung,
where the fog prowls for passersby,
rubs against their hearts, gives a sly
cold reminder of its tongue.

The moon's echoes down there shine
like the eyes of ghosts.
A place where memories are lost;
where emptiness comes padding up behind.

CATHERINE FISHER

HALLOWE'EN

At night we walked the street.
I was wearing my wolf face.

The moon was shining brightly
and I began to howl.

The moon was like a plate.
I howled like a hungry wolf.

I howled and howled and howled,
till I met the lion.

Mask to mask we stood,
and our hair bristled.

IAIN CRICHTON SMITH

HIDE AND SEEK

Call out. Call loud: "I'm ready! Come and find me!"
The sacks in the toolshed smell like the seaside.
They'll never find you in this salty dark,
But be careful that your feet aren't sticking out.
Wiser not to risk another shout.
The floor is cold. They'll probably be searching
The bushes near the swing. Whatever happens
You mustn't sneeze when they come prowling in.
And here they are, whispering at the door;
You've never heard them sound so hushed before.
Don't breathe. Don't move. Stay dumb. Hide in your blindness.
They're moving closer, someone stumbles, mutters;
Their words and laughter scuffle, and they're gone.

But don't come out just yet; they'll try the lane
And then the greenhouse and back here again.
They must be thinking that you're very clever,
Getting more puzzled as they search all over.
It seems a long time since they went away.
Your legs are stiff, the cold bites through your coat;
The dark damp smell of sand moves in your throat.
It's time to let them know that you're the winner.
Push off the sacks. Uncurl and stretch. That's better!
Out of the shed and call to them: "I've won!
Here I am! Come and own up I've caught you!"
The darkening garden watches. Nothing stirs.
The bushes hold their breath; the sun is gone.
Yes, here you are. But where are they who sought you?

VERNON SCANNELL

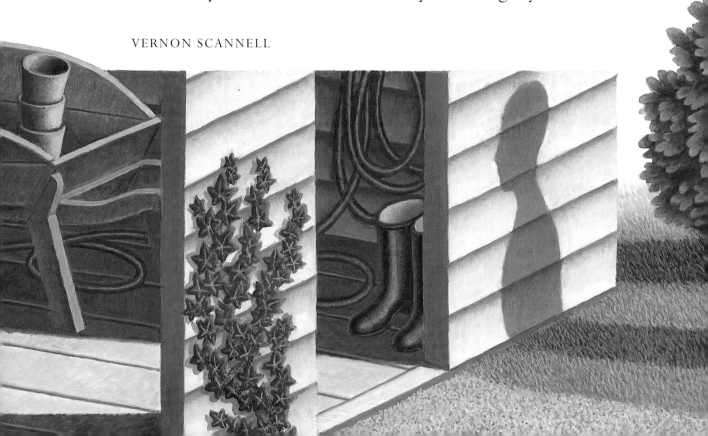

from *THE OWL*

When cats run home and light is come,
   And dew is cold upon the ground,
And the far-off stream is dumb,
   And the whirring sail goes round,
   And the whirring sail goes round;
     Alone and warming his five wits,
     The white owl in the belfry sits.

ALFRED, LORD TENNYSON

HAUNTED

Black hill
black hall
all still
owl's grey cry
edges shrill
castle night.

Woken eye
round in fright;
what lurks walks
in castle rustle?

Hand cold
held hand
the moving roving
urging thing:
dreamed margin

voiceless
noiseless
HEARD
feared
a ghost passed

black hill
black hall
all still
owl's grey cry
edges shrill
castle night.

WILLIAM MAYNE

THE BAT

By day the bat is cousin to the mouse;
He likes the attic of an ageing house.

His fingers make a hat about his head.
His pulse-beat is so slow we think him dead.

He loops in crazy figures half the night
Among the trees that face the corner light.

But when he brushes up against a screen,
We are afraid of what our eyes have seen:

For something is amiss or out of place
When mice with wings can wear a human face.

THEODORE ROETHKE

BATS

Bats like various
musty old areas:

belfries, of course,
where they rehearse

a crotchety score,
dangling galore

from crossbar staves,
troubling graves

with the dark bells' boom
of their leather tune;

or a spooky loft
where dust lies soft

on forgotten things,
and someone sings

in her room below
that song bats know

whose notes contain
the squeak of pain . . .

Oh, bats like various
vicarious areas,

preferably precarious.

JOHN MOLE

I SAW THREE WITCHES

I saw three witches
That bowed down like barley,
And took to their brooms 'neath a louring sky,
And, mounting a storm-cloud,
Aloft on its margin,
Stood black in the silver as up they did fly.

I saw three witches
That mocked the poor sparrows
They carried in cages of wicker along,
Till a hawk from his eyrie
Swooped down like an arrow,
And smote on the cages, and ended their song.

I saw three witches
That sailed in a shallop
All turning their heads with a truculent smile
Till a bank of green osiers
Concealed their grim faces,
Though I heard them lamenting for many a mile.

I saw three witches
Asleep in a valley,
Their heads in a row, like stones in a flood,
Till the moon, creeping upward,
Looked white through the valley,
And turned them to bushes in bright scarlet bud.

WALTER DE LA MARE

THERE CAME A WIND LIKE A BUGLE

There came a Wind like a Bugle –
It quivered through the Grass
And a Green Chill upon the Heat
So ominous did pass
We barred the Windows and the Doors
As from an Emerald Ghost –
The Doom's electric Moccasin
That very instant passed –
On a strange Mob of panting Trees
And Fences fled away
And Rivers where the Houses ran
Those looked that lived – that Day –
The Bell within the steeple wild
The flying tidings told –
How much can come
And much can go,
And yet abide the World!

EMILY DICKINSON

THE KNEE

There wanders through the world, a knee
It's just a knee, no more.
It's not a tent; it's not a tree;
Only a knee, no more.

There was a man once in a war
Overkilled, killed fatally.
Alone, unhurt, remained the knee
Like a saint's relics, pure.

Since then it roams the whole world, lonely.
It is a knee, now, only.
It's not a tent; it's not a tree;
Only a knee, no more.

CHRISTIAN MORGENSTERN

THE SHEPHERD'S HUT

The smear of blue peat smoke
That staggered on the wind and broke,
The only sign of life,
Where was the shepherd's wife,
Who left those flapping clothes to dry,
Taking no thought for her family?
For, as they bellied out
And limbs took shape and waved about,
I thought, She little knows
That ghosts are trying on her children's clothes.

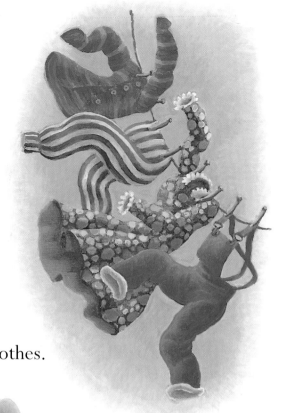

ANDREW YOUNG

THREE LITTLE GHOSTIES

Three little ghosties
Sitting on posties
Eating buttered toasties,
Greasing their fisties
Up to their wristies.

Oh, what beasties,
To have such feasties.

ANON

THE WIND

I saw the wind today:
I saw it in the pane
Of glass upon the wall:

A moving thing, – 'twas like
No bird with widening wing,
No mouse that runs along
The meal bag under the beam.

I think it's like a horse
All black, with frightening mane,
That springs out of the earth,
And tramples on his way.
I saw it in the glass,
The shaking of a mane:
A horse that no one rides.

PADRAIC COLUM

WHO HAS SEEN THE WIND?

Who has seen the wind?
Neither I nor you:
But when the leaves hang trembling,
The wind is passing thro'.
Who has seen the wind?
Neither you nor I:
But when the trees bow down their heads,
The wind is passing by.

CHRISTINA ROSSETTI

SPELLBOUND

The night is darkening round me,
The wild winds coldly blow;
But a tyrant spell has bound me
And I cannot, cannot go.

The giant trees are bending
Their bare boughs weighed with snow.
And the storm is fast descending,
And yet I cannot go.

Clouds beyond clouds above me,
Wastes beyond wastes below;
But nothing drear can move me;
I will not, cannot go.

EMILY BRONTË

NOVEMBER NIGHT

Listen . . .
With faint dry sound,
Like steps of passing ghosts,
The leaves, frost-crisped, break from the trees
And fall.

ADELAIDE CRAPSEY

GHOSTS

A cold and starry darkness moans
   And settles wide and still
Over a jumble of tumbled stones
   Dark on a darker hill.

An owl among those shadowy walls,
   Grey against the grey
Of ruins and brittle weeds, calls
   And soundless swoops away.

Rustling over scattered stones
   Dancers hover and sway,
Drifting among their own bones
   Like webs of the Milky Way.

HARRY BEHN

SONG OF TWO GHOSTS

My friend
This is a wide world
We're travelling over
Walking on the moonlight.

OMAHA INDIAN SONG

WINTER NIGHT

As I lie in bed I hear
The east wind crying in my ear,
And soon will follow, soft and low,
The sifting whisper of the snow.

MARCHETTE CHUTE

61

SNOW WOMAN

A winter's night,
And in the cold outside,
A snow woman forms.

Her icy fingers touch,
Her split snake tongue flickers,
Her evil eyes stare.

Her nails strike down trees,
Her eyes still, and mad.
Night creatures flee.

She grins,
Her laughter echoing.

As a splinter of light
Snatches at her gown
Her feet vanish,
Her ankles, knees and thighs,
Her cackles silenced.

She grabs the empty air,
Her head sliding.
Her hand reaches one last time,
But she is gone.

ELIZABETH HOLDEN
(Aged 10)

THE SNOW

It sifts from Leaden Sieves –
It powders all the Wood.
It fills with Alabaster Wool
The Wrinkles of the Road –

It makes an Even Face
Of Mountain, and of Plain –
Unbroken Forehead from the East
Unto the East again –

It reaches to the Fence –
It wraps it Rail by Rail
Till it is lost in Fleeces –
It deals Celestial Veil

To Stump, and Stack – and Stem –
A Summer's empty Room –
Acres of Joints, where Harvests were,
Recordless, but for them –

It Ruffles Wrists of Posts
As Ankles of a Queen –
Then stills its Artisans – like Ghosts –
Denying they have been –

EMILY DICKINSON

THE FROZEN MAN

Out at the edge of town
where black trees

crack their fingers
in the icy wind

and hedges freeze
on their shadows

and the breath of cattle,
still as boulders,

hangs in rags
under the rolling moon,

a man is walking
alone:

on the coal-black road
his cold

feet
ring

and
ring.

Here in a snug house
at the heart of town

the fire is burning
red and yellow and gold:

you can hear the warmth
like a sleeping cat

breathe softly
in every room.

When the frozen man
comes to the door,

let him in,
let him in,
let him in.

KIT WRIGHT

TRICK OF THE LIGHTS

Late, late at night
you may never get home. They wink the word
from light to light

all down the long straight
empty road. Each one in turn will turn
against you, but they wait

green as grass on the opposite side
of a triptrap bridge, where amber teeth
and bloodshot eyes might hide

as you pedal for home, too fast. Too late.

PHILIP GROSS

CARBREAKERS

There's a graveyard in our street,
But it's not for putting people in;
The bodies that they bury here
Are made of steel and paint and tin.

The people come and leave their wrecks
For crunching in the giant jaws
Of a great hungry car-machine,
That lives on bonnets, wheels and doors.

When I pass by the yard at night,
I sometimes think I hear a sound
Of ghostly horns that moan and whine,
Upon that metal-graveyard mound.

MARIAN LINES

HOUSE FEAR

Always – I tell you this they learned –
Always at night when they returned
To the lonely house from far away
To lamps unlighted and fire gone grey,
They learned to rattle the lock and key
To give whatever might chance to be
Warning and time to be off in flight:
And preferring the out- to the in-door night,
They learned to leave the house-door wide
Until they had lit the lamp inside.

ROBERT FROST

Index of Poets

Index of Titles and First Lines

Titles are in *italics*. Where the title and the first line are the same, the first line only is listed.

Acknowledgements

The publisher would like to thank the copyright holders for permission to reproduce the following copyright material:

Dannie Abse: Sheil Land Associates for "Emperors of the Island" by Dannie Abse. Copyright © Dannie Abse. **John Agard**: John Agard and Caroline Sheldon Literary Agency for "The Speller's Bag" from *Grandfather's Bruk-a-Down Car* by John Agard, Bodley Head 1994. Copyright © John Agard 1994. **Harry Behn**: Marian Reiner Literary Agent for "Ghosts" from *The Golden Hive* by Harry Behn. Copyright © Harry Behn 1957, 1962 and 1966. **Frances Bellerby**: David Higham Associates Ltd for "Voices" from *Selected Poems* by Frances Bellerby, Enitharmon Press. Copyright © Frances Bellerby. **Charles Causley**: David Higham Associates Ltd for "Who?" by Charles Causley. Copyright © Charles Causley. **Marchette Chute**: Elizabeth Roach for "Winter Night" from *Rhymes About Us* by Marchette Chute, E.P. Dutton 1974. Copyright © Marchette Chute 1974. **Marta Jadwiga Ciechanowicz**: The author for "The Old Clock House" by Marta Jadwiga Ciechanowicz. Copyright © Marta Jadwiga Ciechanowicz 1996. **Gillian Clarke**: The author for "The Man in the Wilderness" and "The Titanic" by Gillian Clarke. Copyright © Gillian Clarke 1996. **Walter de la Mare**: The Literary Trustees of Walter de la Mare, and the Society of Authors as their representative for "I Saw Three Witches" from *The Complete Poems of Walter de la Mare*. Copyright © Walter de la Mare. **Berlie Doherty**: Murray Pollinger Literary Agent for "Quieter than Snow" by Berlie Doherty from *Walking on Air*, HarperCollins 1992. Copyright © Berlie Doherty 1991. **Helen Dunmore**: Random House UK Ltd for "The Bones of the Vasa" from *Secrets* by Helen Dunmore, Bodley Head 1994. Copyright © Helen Dunmore 1994. **Catherine Fisher**: The author for "Cat Lane" by Catherine Fisher. Copyright © Catherine Fisher 1996. **Robert Frost**: Random House UK Ltd for "House Fear" from *The Poetry of Robert Frost*, edited by Edward Connery Lathem. Copyright © Robert Frost 1951. **Philip Gross**: The author for "Trick of the Lights" by Philip Gross. Copyright © Philip Gross 1995. **Elizabeth Holden**: W H Smith Ltd for "Snow Woman" by Elizabeth Holden from *Walk the Hire Wire*, the 1994 W H Smith Young Writers' Competition Anthology. **Miroslav Holub**: Penguin Books Ltd for "Water Sprite" from *Miroslav Holub: Selected Poems* by Miroslav Holub, translated by Ian Milner and George Theiner, Penguin Modern Poets 1967. **Ted Hughes**: The author for "Sea Monster" by Ted Hughes. Copyright © Ted Hughes 1995. **Marian Lines**: Franklin Watts for "Carbreakers" by Marian Lines from *Tower Blocks*. Copyright © Marian Lines. **William Mayne**: David Higham Associates Ltd for "Haunted" from *Ghosts: An Anthology*, edited by William Mayne, Hamish Hamilton 1971. Copyright © William Mayne 1971. **Adrian Mitchell**: Peters, Fraser & Dunlop Group Ltd for "The Woman of Water" from *Nothingmas Day* by Adrian Mitchell, Allison & Busby 1984. Copyright © Adrian Mitchell 1984. None of Adrian Mitchell's poems are to be used in any examination whatsoever. **John Mole**: Peterloo Poets for "Bats" by John Mole. Copyright © John Mole. **Christian Morgenstern**: W.D. Snodgrass for "The Knee" from *Gallows Songs* by Christian Morgenstern, translated by Lore Segal and W.D. Snodgrass. **Sue Moules**: The author for "The Other Life" by Sue Moules. Copyright © Sue Moules 1996. **Judith Nicholls**: Faber & Faber Ltd for "Night" from *Magic Mirror and Other Poems for Children* by Judith Nicholls, Faber & Faber 1985. Copyright © Judith Nicholls 1985. **Grace Nichols**: Penguin Books Ltd for "Mama-Wata" by Grace Nichols from *No Hickory, No Dickory, No Dock* by Grace Nichols and John Agard, Viking 1991. Copyright © Grace Nichols 1991. **Omaha Indian**: Columbia University Press for "Song of Two Ghosts" from *Omaha Secret Societies* by R.F. Fortune. Copyright © Columbia University Press 1932. **Jack Prelutsky**: Greenwillow Books, a division of William Morrow & Co. Inc., for "The Bogeyman" from *Nightmares* by Jack Prelutsky. Copyright © Jack Prelutsky 1976. **James Reeves**: Laura Cecil Literary Agency on behalf of the James Reeves Estate for "The Sea" from *The Complete Poems for Children* by James Reeves, Heinemann 1975. Copyright © James Reeves 1975. **John Rice**: The author for "A Sweep of Ghosts" by John Rice. Copyright © John Rice 1996. **Theodore Roethke**: A.M. Heath & Co. Ltd for "The Bat" from *The Waking: Poems 1933-1935* by Theodore Roethke. Copyright © The late Theodore Roethke. **Andrew Salkey**: Patricia Salkey for "Anancy" by Andrew Salkey. Copyright © Andrew Salkey. **Carl Sandburg**: Harcourt Brace & Company for "Theme in Yellow" from *Chicago Poems* by Carl Sandburg. Copyright © Holt, Rinehart and Winston, Inc. and renewed by Carl Sandburg 1944. **Vernon Scannell**: The author for "Hide and Seek" from *Walking Wounded* by Vernon Scannell, Eyre & Spottiswoode 1965. Copyright © Vernon Scannell 1965. **Ian Serraillier**: Anne Serraillier for "The Visitor" by Ian Serraillier. Copyright © Ian Serraillier. **Ian Crichton Smith**: Carcanet Press Ltd for "Hallowe'en" from *Collected Poems* by Ian Crichton Smith, Carcanet 1992. Copyright © Ian Crichton Smith 1992. **Stevie Smith**: James MacGibbon for "Fairy Story" from *The Collected Poems of Stevie Smith* by Stevie Smith, Penguin 20th Century Classics. Copyright © The Estate of Stevie Smith 1972. **Efua Sutherland**: The author for "Song of the Fishing Ghosts" by Efua Sutherland. Copyright © Efua Sutherland. **Kit Wright**: HarperCollins Publishers Ltd for "The Frozen Man" from *Rabbiting On* by Kit Wright. Copyright © Kit Wright 1978. **Andrew Young**: The Andrew Young Estate for "The Shepherd's Hut" from *The Poetical Works of Andrew Young*, edited by Edward Lowbury and Alison Young, Secker & Warburg 1985. Copyright © Andrew Young.

Every effort has been made to obtain permission to reproduce copyright material but there may be cases where we have been unable to trace a copyright holder. The publisher will be happy to correct any omissions in future printings.